That's
the
Trick!

That's the Trick!

Krista Bell and Sarah Dunk

Lothian
BOOKS

Lothian Books
An imprint of Hachette Livre Australia
132 Albert Road, South Melbourne, Victoria 3205
www.lothian.com.au

First published 2006
Reprinted 2006

National Library of Australia
Cataloguing-in-Publication data:

Bell, Krista.
    That's the trick.

    For children.
    ISBN 0 7344 0894 3.

    1. Homonyms. I. Dunk, Sarah. II. Title.

413.1

Cover design by Michelle Mackintosh
Text design by Paulene Meyer
Printed in Australia by Griffin Press

WHY I WROTE THIS BOOK

I love words, **but** English spelling can **be** tricky. As an author **I** travel **right** around Australia giving writing workshops, **so I know** that homophones (also called homonyms) cause **real** problems.

Homophones are words that sound the same, but are usually spelt differently and mean different things; for example: **to**, **too**, **two**.

When **I** decided **to write** a book **to** illustrate the differences between homophones **I** first had **to** make a word list of up **to** 300 homophones. Luckily my brother, Mike Blakeney, loves words **too**, **so we** had months and months of fun collecting the homophones **for** this book, which is dedicated **to** Mike, with love and thanks.

Once the word list was ready, **I** worked with Andrew Davies and his Years 5/6 students (2005) at St Mary's Primary School, East Malvern. **I** thank them **for their** infectious humour which **made** our sessions together **so** much fun. Each of them is a crazy character **in** this book.

I must also thank the countless teachers and librarians who over **two** years generously checked and added **to** my word list as **I** travelled around the country, especially Brigid, Toni, Julie and Sally at St Mary's; Anne, Elaine, John, Anne, Lois and Judy at Swan Hill Primary School; Lisa, Keilly and Judy at Weetangera Primary School (ACT); and Sue Norris and Yvonne Kamholtz **in** Gladstone, Queensland. I'm indebted **to you** all, as **I** am to my editor, Gwenda Smyth, a true wordsmith.

Enjoy reading *That's the Trick*, and when **you** find other homophones that are **not in** this book, **write** them down on the blank pages at the back. Perhaps you'd like **to** email them **to** me **too**, via my homepage. You'll **be** surprised just how many are lurking out **there**, waiting **to** trick **you**!

Krista Bell
www.kristabell.com

Aa

ad, add

It doesn't take Jack long to do the TV **ad** for beanstalks, but it takes him ages to **add** up all the magic beans he's been paid.

addition, edition

As the first **edition** of the paper was
about to go to press, the
editor made a late
addition to the
front-page
news.

affect, effect

The painter used dark colours to create
a dramatic **effect**, but it seemed to
affect everyone so badly that
they cried.

aisle, I'll, isle

One day **I'll** walk down the **aisle** of a church, get married and then honeymoon on a tropical **isle**.

allowed, aloud

The prince is not **allowed** to burp **aloud**, so he does it quietly and avoids trouble.

altar, alter

The nun had to **alter** the position of the statue, because the **altar** was covered with flowers.

ate, eight

Jaimie-Lee's dog **ate** her homework — first he ripped up all **eight** pages and then he swallowed them.

awe, oar, or, ore

Dan watched in **awe** as the pirate loaded the boat with silver **ore**, then picked up an **oar** and rowed away — **or** was it all a dream?

aye, eye, I

'**Aye**, **aye**, captain!' yelled the pirate. '**I** will keep my one good **eye** on this here pesky parrot!'

Bb

bail, bale

Because he had stolen a **bale** of hay, Cock Robin was refused **bail** and sent to jail.

bald, bawled

When the hairdresser shaved off Michael's
feathers so that he was **bald**, the
big fellow **bawled** like a baby.

ball, bawl

Humpty Dumpty started to **bawl** when he
tripped over a **ball** and had a great fall.

band, band, banned

Because Joshua flicked a rubber **band** at his sister, he was **banned** from listening to his favourite music, the Big Green Whale **Band**.

bare, bear, bear

The cheeky brown **bear** flashed his **bare** bottom at the passing cars as he skateboarded to the underpants shop, unable to **bear** the cold any longer.

base, bass

Playing her **bass** guitar with her eyes shut,
Alyssa accidentally smashed
the **base** of her mother's
favourite lamp.

be, bee

To **be** a busy **bee** or not to **be** a busy **bee** —
that is the question!

beach, beech

After plodding through the **beech** tree forest,
the walkers had a swim at the **beach**.

bean, been

The little **bean** had **been** on his way to
Queensland to see the Big Baked **Bean** when a
hungry crow swallowed him.

beat, beet

Grandma grated the fresh **beet** into the bowl,
beat in some flour and
eggs, and made a
red cake.

berry, bury

When the elf found the big, red **berry**,
he decided to **bury** it
in the soil to see
if it would grow
into a tree.

berth, birth

Captain Hook steered his boat into its **berth** at the marina, while below decks Mrs Hook gave **birth** to their seventh child.

bight, bite, byte

Researching his school project, Andrew took a **bite** of his sandwich as he downloaded a 300-kilo**byte** image of the Great Australian **Bight**.

billed, build

When you **build** a new house you might get **billed** for lots of extra bits and pieces.

blew, blue

Isabella **blew** up so many balloons for the party that she went **blue** in the face.

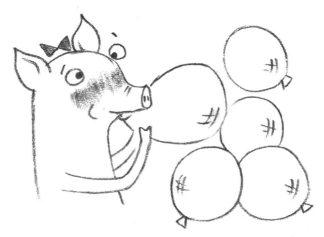

boar, bore, bore

The piglets thought old grandpa **boar** was a
total **bore** when he bragged about how his
tusks could **bore**
holes in the
ground.

board, bored

Emily was so **bored** that she tidied her room
and made a pin-up **board** for her favourite
pictures.

boarder, border

The mysterious **boarder** who rents the spare
room fled across the **border** from
another country.

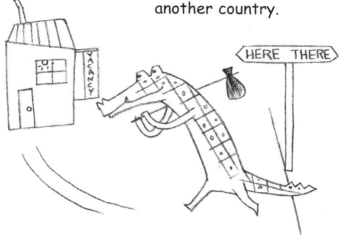

bold, bowled

The **bold** girl rudely snatched the ball from
her teacher and **bowled** it down the alley.

bolder, boulder

Little Miss Muffet was shy when she climbed onto the **boulder**, but she became **bolder** as she told the crowd about the spider.

bough, bow

After the penguin had tap-danced along the **bough** of the tree, he took a **bow** and everybody clapped.

boy, buoy

Every day that **boy** swims out to the floating **buoy** and back, as part of his training.

braid, brayed

The donkey **brayed** as he happily chewed the **braid** off Tim's school blazer.

brake, break

As Humpty Dumpty slammed on the **brake**, he
shut his eyes and wondered if
he'd hit the wall and **break**
into small pieces.

bread, bred

The loaf of **bread** was so old that it **bred** some
very strange creatures.

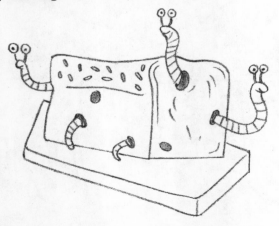

brewed, brood, brood

While her pot of coffee **brewed** on the stove, Mrs Bunny told her large **brood** of children not to **brood** over spilt milk.

bridal, bridle

The **bridal** couple each wore a fancy **bridle** as they raced down the aisle to get hitched.

but, butt

The bull tried to **butt** Farmer Brown into the next paddock **but** he missed and got his horns stuck in the fence.

buy, by, bye

As Sophie had a **bye** in netball and didn't have to play, she went to the shops **by** bus to **buy** some new clothes.

Cc

calves, calves, carves

As Mrs Sprat **carves** the roast for dinner, with the cat rubbing hungrily against her **calves**, she hears the **calves** mooing in the paddock.

caught, court, court

Instead of playing tennis on her friend's **court**, Goldilocks had to face the judge in **court** because she had been **caught** stealing porridge.

cause, caws

The concert was for a good **cause**, so the audience put up with the screeching **caws** of the Crow Brothers.

ceiling, sealing

Ethan's mother found him **sealing** his pesky little brother into the hole in the family room **ceiling**.

cell, sell

The Wicked Witch was just about to **sell** one of her poisonous apples when the policeman came and locked her up in a jail **cell**.

cellar, seller

Jessica's uncle is a
shoe **seller** and he
keeps his stock in
the **cellar** under
his house.

cent, scent, sent

Jordie spent every **cent** he had buying an
expensive bottle of **scent** which he **sent** to his
girlfriend for
her birthday.

cents, scents

The queen spent lots of **cents** hiring a sniffer
dog to pick up the **scents** of the knaves
who stole the tarts.

cereal, serial

Instead of having **cereal**, Little Red Riding
Hood ate eggs for breakfast, while she
watched her favourite TV **serial**, "Lost in the
Wood".

cheap, cheep

The girls went to the fair and bought some **cheap** tickets to see the Singing Chicken, but all it did was go "**Cheep, cheep, cheep**".

chews, choose

Old Mother Hubbard **chews** a chocolate muffin as she opens the cupboard to **choose** a bone for her dog.

Chile, chilli, chilly

Zoe visited **Chile**, a South
American country with
chilly mountains and
spicy food made
with red-hot
chilli peppers.

choral, coral

The fish sang together in a **choral** group as
they danced through the **coral** reef.

chord, cord, cored

The circus monkey could play a guitar **chord**
while he **cored** an
apple hanging
on a **cord**.

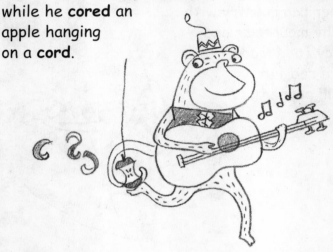

chute, shoot

To **shoot** his dirty clothes
down the **chute** into the
laundry basket, Liam
rolls them up
into a ball.

cite, sight, site

At the **site** where he catches **sight** of Little
Boy Blue, the farmer begins to **cite** the rhyme:
"Where's the boy who looks after the sheep?"

Claus, clause, claws

Santa **Claus** made his cat sign a document with
a **clause** that promised it would never, ever
sharpen its **claws** on the sleigh again.

coarse, course

The gravel under the model railway line was so **coarse** that it made the toy train go off **course** and crash.

colonel, kernel

When **Colonel** Custer made his last stand at Little Big Horn, he munched on some popcorn and cracked his tooth on an unpopped **kernel**.

complement, compliment

The judges paid the competitors a **compliment**,
saying that they danced together very well
and were the perfect
complement for
each other.

coo, coup

As his new pigeons began to **coo** happily in the
dovecot, Lachlan knew he had pulled off a
major **coup** in buying this pair
of champion birds.

core, corps

Three nurses from the medical **corps** were trying to remove the apple **core** that was stuck in the captain's throat.

council, counsel

The town **council** employed someone to **counsel** the residents who had lost their homes in the bushfire.

creak, creek

Daisy heard the rope **creak**
on the tree branch
just before it broke
and she fell into the
icy **creek**.

crews, cruise

The **crews** of the tugboats waved goodbye to
the travellers who were going on an island
cruise aboard the ocean liner.

cue, queue

It's difficult to pee on **cue** when there's
a **queue** forming behind you.

curb, kerb

When a skateboarder did a grind on the **kerb**,
Hannah pulled hard on the leash to **curb** her dog.

currant, current, current

On the **current** affairs programme there was a
story about the river **current** sweeping away
a load of **currant** buns.

cymbal, symbol

When the drummer tried out his noisy new
cymbal, the Big Green Whale thought it should
be the **symbol** on the band's
new banner!

Dd

days, daze

Henny Penny was in such a **daze** that she bumped into a tree, knocked herself out and spent five **days** recovering in hospital.

dear, dear, deer

When Santa was away on holidays he sent a postcard: "**Dear** Rudolph, you are my favourite **deer**. This hotel is very **dear**. Can't afford to stay long!"

dew, due, due

Due to the pixie's carelessness, the book that was **due** back to the elf library today was left out on a toadstool all night and is wet with **dew**.

died, dyed

When Rachel walked into the classroom with her hair **dyed** purple, the little mouse got such a surprise that it **died** of shock.

discussed, disgust

After the boys had **discussed** swapping lunches, Steve walked away in **disgust** because he'd been given a broccoli burger.

doe, doh, dough

Mrs Bambi is a very busy **doe** making **dough** for her famous berry pies, as she sings her favourite tune, **doh**-ray-me-fah-soh-lah-te-**doh**.

draft, draught

Thomas had just printed out the first **draft** of his story, when a **draught** of wind blew the pages right out the window.

dual, duel

When the family left the **dual**-carriage highway and turned down a country road, they saw two teddy bears fighting a **duel**.

Ee

earn, urn

When the black cat smashed
a precious **urn**, she had to
earn enough money to
buy a new one.

ewe, yew, you

The hungry **ewe** and her lamb were munching grass near the **yew** tree, when the farmer yelled: 'Hey, **you**, get off my property!'

ewes, use, yews

The day Little Bo Peep lost all her **ewes** she needed to **use** her hand-held GPS before she found them hiding among the **yews**.

Ff

faint, feint

The footballer tried to **feint** a move to the
left to trick his opponent, but when they
bumped heads he felt as though he might **faint**.

fair, fair, fair, fare

It wasn't **fair** — after Nikita paid
her **fare** to get to the **fair** she
heard that if you had **fair**
hair you got in for half
price!

farther, father

Robin Hood's **father** wondered how much
farther into the woods his little boy would go
to build his tree-house.

fate, fête

Because Sammy was the best swimmer, he knew it would be his **fate** to sit on the dunking chair at the school **fête**.

faux, foe

Paige defeated her **foe** in the fashion contest by making a stunning coat out of **faux** fur that only a fox would know was fake.

faze, phase

Sarah is going through a healthy eating **phase** when nothing can **faze** her, even a huge plate of green vegetables.

feat, feet

The judges said the winner had performed an amazing **feat** by painting his picture with the brush held in his **feet**.

few, phew

Phew, it was hot! The bike riders were thankful that there were only a **few** others in the cold drinks queue.

find, fined

When the police **find** the creature who stole the seeing-eye cat from the Three Blind Mice, the thief will be **fined** for the crime.

fir, fur

Matthew knew he was on track to the Easter
Bunny's house when he found some
rabbit **fur** caught on the low
branch of a
fir tree.

flair, flare

Everyone thought Maddie's **flair** for fashion
was useless out in the bush, until they got lost
and she took a signal **flare** out of
her designer handbag.

flaw, floor

The bump in the middle of
the **floor** wasn't a **flaw**
in the new rug — it
was Turtle playing
hide-and-seek.

flea, flee

The fire-fighting **flea** jumped to the rescue of
his friends who were trying to **flee** from the
fire in the lost dogs' home.

flecks, flex

As the audience watched Tarzan **flex** his muscles,
they noticed **flecks** of dandruff
falling to the ground.

flew, flu, flue

When Rudolph was sick with the
flu he was so confused that
he **flew** up the chimney
flue and got stuck.

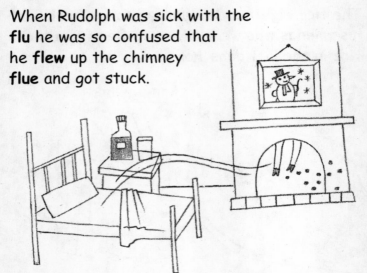

flour, flower

Ebony knew that every **flower** on the bush would produce seeds that she could grind into **flour** to make her special bread.

for, fore, four

The King came to the **fore** as a nursery rhyme favourite when there were **four** and twenty blackbirds baked in a pie **for** his dinner.

fort, fought

The cowboys **fought** the Indians from the walls of the **fort** until Sitting Bull got a headache and had to go home.

forth, fourth

The **fourth** line in our school play is "go **forth** and find the stinky cheese", so we pretend to go and look for it.

foul, fowl

Chased by the fox, the terrified **fowl** flew into an electric fence and clucked in **foul** language, saying this was **foul** play.

frees, freeze, frieze

Spider Mouse **frees** himself from his cage and runs up the wall to the wallpaper **frieze**, when Samuel yells: "**Freeze**! That's as far as you go!"

Gg

gait, gate

Black Beauty changed his **gait** from a trot to a canter and easily jumped the paddock **gate**.

genes, jeans

Because Grace inherited Irish **genes** from her grandparents, she likes to wear green **jeans** and T-shirt on St Patrick's Day.

gilt, guilt

When the silly maid broke the Queen's **gilt** crown, she felt such terrible **guilt** that she tried to fix it with bread and honey.

gnaw, nor

The guard dog could not **gnaw** through the fence, **nor** could he climb it.

grade, greyed

When the whole **grade** failed the exam, their teacher's hair **greyed** overnight.

grate, great

The Big Green Whale said that Ana was a **great** girl because she was always happy to **grate** fresh Parmesan cheese onto his spaghetti bolognaise.

graze, greys

The painting of the cow that likes to **graze** in Farmer Brown's paddock was very dull with too many **greys** and not enough bright colours.

grease, Greece

When Luke stepped off the ferry in **Greece**, he slipped on a patch of car **grease** and fell into Athens harbour.

grill, grille

The silly elf tried to **grill** his lunch on the barbecue, but most of it dropped through the **grille** onto the hot coals.

groan, grown

The class heard Steph **groan** when Mr Davies measured her height and she hadn't **grown** even one millimetre.

groin, groyne

As Rhys did his warm-up run along the beach to the **groyne**, he pulled his **groin** muscle and couldn't go surfing.

guessed, guest

The Three Bears could never have **guessed** that they would have such a famous **guest**.

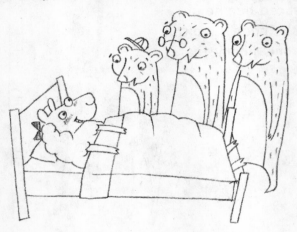

gym, Jim

Every day after school **Jim** goes to the health club to work out in the **gym**.

Hh

hail, hale

The golfers were feeling **hale** and hearty until **hail** the size of golf balls knocked them over.

hair, hare

On cue Rapunzel let down her long, plaited **hair**, but a **hare** ran up it instead of a prince.

hall, hall, haul

The little ant could not easily **haul** the loaf of bread from the dining **hall** down the **hall** to his hole, but he got there in the end.

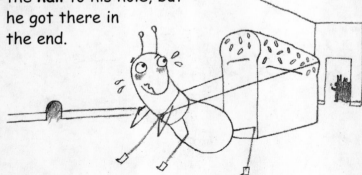

hangar, hanger

The pilot was so busy putting his coat on a **hanger** that he crashed his plane into the door of its **hangar**.

hay, hey

Hey diddle diddle the cat did a piddle and the cow jumped over the smelly bale of wet **hay**.

heal, heel, he'll

If Nicholas wants to train that dog to **heel**
properly, **he'll** have to wait for its
broken leg to **heal**.

hear, here

The principal was standing right **here** talking to
Peter, but Peter couldn't **hear** a word because
he had a carrot in each ear.

heard, herd

The tourists thought they **heard** thunder, but it was a **herd** of wild elephants heading straight for them.

hi, high

Superfly said "**Hi**" and waved to all the office workers as he climbed **high** up the side of the skyscraper.

higher, hire

The trekkers decided to **hire** a four-wheel drive so they could go **higher** into the mountains.

him, hymn

Because the choir leader told **him** he had a good voice, Harrison was happy to sing the **hymn** in church.

hoard, horde

Santa's **hoard** of chocolate disappeared when the hungry **horde** arrived home after the football game.

hoarse, horse

The adults yelled so loudly at the **horse** races that they were **hoarse** by the end of the day.

hoes, hose

The Seven Dwarfs were using their **hoes** to tidy up Snow White's garden, when they accidentally chopped her **hose** in half.

hold, holed

Once the iceberg had **holed** her boat, the Little Mermaid could no longer **hold** it on course, so she jumped ship.

hole, whole

The **whole** school wondered who had put the **hole** in the window until they saw the Big Green Whale holding a bat and laughing.

holey, holy, wholly

Because he was wearing **holey** clothes that were **wholly** unacceptable, William was refused entry to the **holy** church ruins.

hour, our

Sometimes we forget what **hour** it is when we're playing on the beach and we get home late for **our** dinner.

humerus, humorous

Pinocchio didn't find it at all **humorous** when he tripped over his nose and broke his **humerus**.

Ii

idle, idol

The new teen **idol** doesn't mind that he has no time to be **idle**, because his life as a pop star is a dream come true.

in, inn

When they arrived at the **inn**, the travellers were shocked to hear there were no rooms left **in** which they could sleep.

it's, its

It's cool when a nasty smell escapes and does **its** best to stink out the classroom.

Jj

jam, jamb

Little Miss Muffet put a large tin of plum **jam** against the door to keep it open while she painted the timber door **jamb**.

Kk

key, quay

As Ruby put the **key** in her front door, she remembered that she'd left her umbrella on the wharf at Circular **Quay**.

knead, need

If you hope to be a successful baker, you **need** to learn how to **knead** the dough so your bread will rise.

knew, new

The shoemaker **knew** that without help from the elves he could never have made such beautiful **new** shoes.

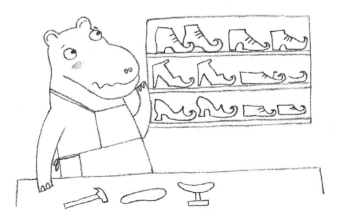

knight, night

As he rode his horse to King Arthur's castle that cold **night**, the brave **knight** had a hot water bottle inside his armour.

knit, nit

Sitting in the Billy Goat Gruff's long hairy coat, the little **nit** got out its needles and started to **knit** itself a scarf.

knot, not

Emma knew that she would **not** remember to turn off the oven, so she put a **knot** in her hair to remind herself.

know, no

Dylan wants to **know** why there are **no** tickets left for The Big Green Whale Band's concert.

knows, noes, nose

Sniffy **knows** that he has a great **nose** for finding things even though, when the handlers voted, the **noes** won and Sniffy had to leave sniffer dog school.

Ll

lacks, lax

The rules are so **lax** that the school **lacks** all discipline.

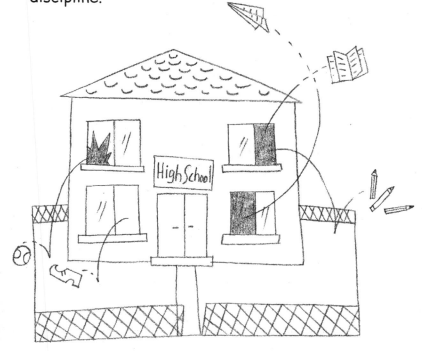

law, lore

Even though Ned
Kelly broke the **law**,
he's a legend in
bushranger **lore**.

Hall of Fame

lays, laze, leis

At the hotel in Hawaii, the manager **lays**
beautiful flower **leis** around the guests' necks
and suggests they go **laze** beside the pool.

lead, led

Simple Simon knew that no one could play music on that rusty **lead** pipe, so he **led** his friends away from the silly competition.

leak, leek

When Peter Rabbit's mother made a pot of delicious **leek** soup, she didn't expect it to **leak** all over the table.

leant, lent, Lent

Wearing the Easter bonnet his sister
had **lent** him, James **leant** against
the tree and dreamed
of all the chocolate
he'd eat after **Lent**.

leased, least

Painting the house was the **least** of Alexander's
worries — he had to get it **leased** to tenants
before he could go on holidays.

lessen, lesson

The famous chef said he would not teach the cooking **lesson** unless they would **lessen** the number of students from thirty to fifteen.

liar, lyre

The musician was a **liar** to tell the audience his **lyre** had broken strings, when he had actually sold it.

licence, license

The policeman said that although Vonnie had a **licence** to fish, the certificate didn't **license** her to catch every fish in the dam.

lightening, lightning

Henny Penny was just **lightening** her backpack by removing some of the rocks she'd collected, when a **lightning** flash lit up the sky.

loan, lone

The **lone** cowboy knew it
would be quicker if he
got a **loan** of a horse,
instead of waiting
all day for a train.

Station

loch, lock

The captain had to **lock** his steering wheel in
place so he could have a cup of tea as his boat
sailed up the **loch**.

Mm

made, maid

While the **maid** was hanging out the clothes, she wore a scarecrow hat and **made** sure the blackbirds stayed away.

mail, male

Male kangaroos are good boxers, but female kangaroos are better posties because they can keep the **mail** dry.

main, mane

As she galloped bareback down the **main** street of town, Gwendolen hung on to her horse's **mane**.

maize, maze

Little Boy Blue planted a field of **maize** that formed a crazy **maze** in which he got lost.

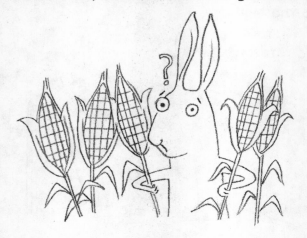

manner, manor

The **manner** in which Mrs Scales opened the door made the TV crew think she was the owner of the **manor** house.

mare, mayor

The bossy stallion wanted to be **mayor** of the village and he was cross with the chestnut **mare** when she won more votes.

marshal, martial

It was so busy at the **martial** arts display that Damien had to **marshal** everyone into lines to wait for their turn.

meat, meet

The Three Little Pigs were scared they would **meet** Mrs Wolf in the woods and end up being the **meat** on her dinner table

medal, meddle

Ryan's sister tended to **meddle** in his business at the football club because she thought he should win the **medal** for best and fairest.

VOTES

BEST & FAIREST

meter, metre

The Big Green Whale had so much to buy that it was lucky he got a parking **meter** only one **metre** away from the shop.

might, mite

The dust **mite** tried really hard in the hope that he **might** make it up the huge hill.

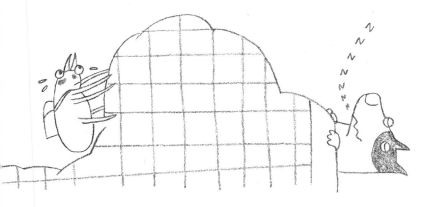

mind, mined

When Tin Man **mined**
his own backyard
looking for a heart,
he didn't **mind**
when he found
gold instead.

miner, minor, mynah

While the **miner** was digging a trench,
a **minor** rockslide trapped
a **mynah** bird by one
of its wings.

missed, mist

Because the **mist** was so thick, no one **missed**
Tyson when he got lost on the
walk in the rainforest.

moan, mown

Dumbo gave a loud **moan** when his father asked
him to wash the car, because he had just **mown**
all the lawns.

mode, mowed

During the bus strike,
Ellie chose an unusual
mode of transport
and **mowed** her
way to work.

moor, more

There were **more** ghosts dancing out on the
spooky **moor** than there were in the cemetery.

morning, mourning

That **morning** when Humpty Dumpty fell off the wall, the whole town went into **mourning** for the popular egg.

muscle, mussel

A **mussel** named Russell flexes his **muscle** and wins the strongman medal.

mustard, mustered

The cunning spider **mustered** the helpless ants towards the **mustard** pot.

Nn

naval, navel

During the **naval** parade, the captain saw that one sailor had a diamond stud in her **navel**.

none, nun

When the priest went to the convent to find a **nun** to help him with the fête, he found there were **none** available.

Oo

ode, owed

Cathy called her poem "An **Ode** to Fish and Chips" because she **owed** its inspiration to her favourite food.

officers, offices,

After the old police station burnt down, the **officers** hoped they would get nice new **offices** to work in.

oh, owe

'**Oh** dear,' said Mother Hubbard to her dog. 'I'll have to **owe** you that bone.'

one, won

Laura **won** the billycart race
because she was the
only **one** in it.

Pp

paced, paste

The teacher **paced** up and down, worried that the students would spill **paste** on the floor.

packed, pact

As they **packed** their bags to go overseas, the two friends made a **pact** that they would both return home in six months.

pail, pale

When Jack dropped the **pail** and fell down the hill, Jill's face went **pale** and she fainted.

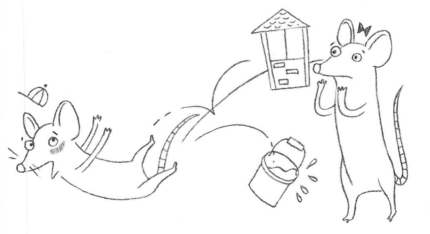

pain, pane

Georgie felt a sharp **pain** in her side, lost her footing and crashed through the **pane** of glass.

pair, pare, pear

The **pair** of friends each took a **pear** and began to **pare** them with a knife to make fruit salad.

passed, past

In the **past** it had been a long walk to Grandma's, but, now that the old lady lived in town, Red Riding Hood **passed** by her house every day.

pause, paws

As Puss-in-Boots put his brand-new boots on his back **paws**, he just had to **pause** and admire them.

paw, poor, pore, pour

Just as the **poor** mother put her **paw** through the window to steal some meat, it began to **pour** with rain and soaked every **pore** of her body.

pea, pee

When the Owl and the Pussycat went to sea in a beautiful **pea**-green boat they had to **pee** over the side into the ocean.

peace, piece

The only way Mr Davies could get any **peace** was to give everybody a **piece** of his chocolate cake.

peak, peek, pique

Reaching the **peak** of the mountain first, Jake took a **peek** at those behind him and knew it would **pique** them if he waved his flag in victory.

peal, peel

There was a **peal** of laughter
as the apple **peel** flew
into the air.

pearl, purl

After she had knitted the cape in plain-and-**purl**
stitch, the Little Mermaid used a rare black
pearl to button it.

pedal, peddle

The Pie Man had to **pedal** his bicycle a long way to the fair in order to **peddle** his wares and earn some money.

peer, pier

When Alice got to the end of the **pier** she had to **peer** into the mist to see if the ferry was coming.

plain, plane

The food served on the **plane** was such **plain** cooking that most of the passengers brought their own meals.

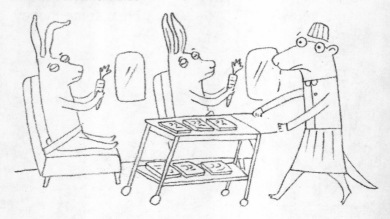

pleas, please

The Billy Goat's **pleas** to be allowed across the bridge didn't **please** the mean old troll.

pole, poll

The mayor took a **poll** to find out how
many people wanted
a new flag **pole**
in the town
square.

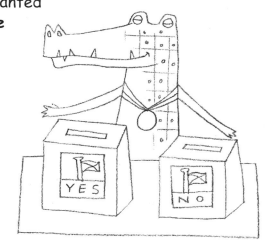

practice, practise

Henry went to football **practice** every
week to **practise** his ball skills
so he'd become a champion.

praise, prays

Before her children go hunting, Mrs Crocodile always **prays** that they'll do well, so she can **praise** their efforts afterwards.

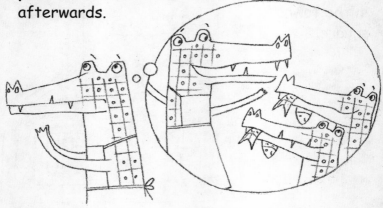

pray, prey

As the keepers return the young geese to the wild, they **pray** that they will not become the **prey** of hawks and eagles.

principal, principle

The **principal** refused to change her mind about the class detention, because it was a matter of **principle**.

profit, prophet

So he would sell lots of tickets and make a big **profit**, the speaker pretended he was a **prophet** and could foretell the future.

Rr

racket, racquet

After their win, the team made such a **racket** that the coach held up his tennis **racquet** to quieten them.

rain, reign, rein

During her **reign** as festival princess, Filomena got so wet in the **rain** that the **rein** slipped out of her hand and the horse bolted.

raise, rays, raze

The demolition crew had to **raise** their hands against the sun's bright **rays** as they checked out the building they had to **raze** to the ground.

rapped, rapt, wrapped

The teacher **rapped** crossly on the locked door, but she was **rapt** when she saw that the class had **wrapped** up a present for her.

raw, roar

At dinner the twins didn't like the **raw** meat and gave a loud **roar** to say so.

read, red

The swimmer's face went **red** when he got out of the pool and **read** the sign.

read, reed

There are some interesting stories to **read** in the Bible, as when Moses was found in a **reed** basket.

real, reel

As Tom hauled in the fish, he got a **real** shock when the **reel** flew off his fishing rod into the ocean.

reek, wreak

If they don't shower after the game, the footballers **reek** of sweat and then **wreak** havoc with their fans.

right, rite, write

You were **right** — Stravinsky did **write** the ballet, The **Rite** of Spring.

ring, wring

The maid had to **wring** the clothes so tightly that her wedding **ring** fell off her finger into the tub.

road, rode, rowed

The Three Little Kittens **rode** their bikes down the **road** to the river and then **rowed** their boat around all afternoon.

roam, Rome

Pinocchio didn't like to **roam** too far from home because the loved the pasta made in **Rome**.

role, roll

The actor was so happy when he got the film **role** that he had a lovely **roll** in the sand.

root, route

Sitting on the **root** of a tree, the Gingerbread Man read the map and worked out the best **route** to escape from the fox.

rose, rows

When the ballet was over, **rows** and **rows** of people all threw a **rose** onto the stage for the principal dancers.

rote, wrote

The class **wrote** a poem about their school camp and learnt it by **rote** to recite on speech night.

rough, ruff

For the play Lauren had to wear a **ruff** around her neck, but the lace was so **rough** it scratched her skin.

rung, wrung

When Jack Sprat slipped on the bottom **rung** of the ladder and broke the window pane, his wife could have **wrung** his neck.

Ss

sacks, sax

On moving day the Pied Piper put all his instruments into **sacks** except for his alto **sax** which he carried.

sail, sale

When the Big Green Whale heard that cheap tuna was on **sale**, he borrowed a boat and set **sail** for Tasmania.

sauce, source

The tortoise believed that his energy **source** was the homemade tomato **sauce** he had eaten before the race.

saw, soar, sore

The ringmaster **saw** his star duck, despite its
sore wing, **soar** past the door of the circus tent.

scene, seen

After checking the **scene** of the
crime, the policeman
nabbed a suspect
who had been
seen running
away.

sea, see

The Big Green Whale laughs because he can **see**
a playful dolphin chasing a jellyfish
out to **sea**.

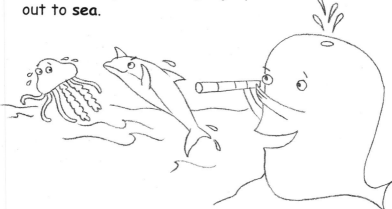

seam, seem

It did **seem** that the champion skateboarder
would win, until he split the **seam** of his pants.

seas, sees, seize

Captain Hook sails the seven **seas** looking for pirates until he **sees** a boat full of treasure that he must **seize**.

sew, so, soh, sow

So that Jenna can **sow** the crop in one day, she decides to **sew** a special bag to hold the seeds and as she sews she hums doh-ray-me-fah-**soh**-lah-te-doh.

shear, sheer

When it was time
to **shear** the sheep,
Little Bo Peep
wondered if some
of them had fallen
over the **sheer**
precipice.

shoe, shoo

Every time Sam tried to visit the children who
lived in a **shoe**, the Old Woman would **shoo**
him away.

shore, sure

As Madison was a champion swimmer, she was quite **sure** that she could swim from the boat to the **shore**.

side, sighed

Little Bo Peep **sighed** with relief when she found her sheep by the **side** of the shearing shed.

sighs, size

No one heard the loud **sighs** as Goldilocks tried to start the motorbike which was not the right **size** for her.

slay, sleigh

Santa looked as if he was going to **slay** a dragon when he drove his **sleigh** dressed as a Viking warrior.

soared, sword

The challenger's hopes **soared** as he knocked the champion's **sword** out of his hands.

sold, soled

As soon as the elf had **soled** the new shoes with leather, the shoemaker **sold** them to a customer.

sole, soul

Old King Cole's **sole** aim in life
was to be a merry old
soul — and yes, he was
a happy chappie!

some, sum

When Mitchell tried to do the **sum** for his
maths homework, he knew there had to be **some**
other way of working it out.

son, sun

Because the family was on holidays, the **son** and daughter were allowed to stay up all night to watch the **sun** rise.

sort, sought

After the food fight the teacher said that was not the **sort** of behaviour she **sought** from her class.

spade, spayed

Before she was **spayed**, Girlie had a litter of
puppies that dug up the garden and chewed
the handle off the **spade**.

stair, stare

Catherine was so shocked that she could only
sit on the **stair** and **stare** at the burnt-out
building.

stake, steak

The **steak** was so tough that the chef put some sauce on a wooden garden **stake** and served that instead.

stationary, stationery

When his carriage was **stationary**, the Emperor bought some **stationery** from the newsagent, so he could write a letter to his tailors.

steal, steel

It was impossible for Ned Kelly to **steal**
the money from the bank because
the doors of the vault were
made of **steel**.

storey, story

After watching the demolition of the old
hospital, one **storey** at a time, the reporter went
back to the newspaper office to write her **story**.

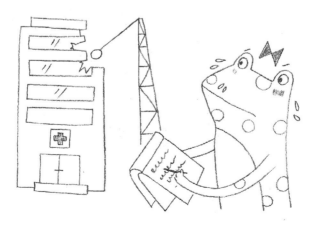

straight, strait

The Tasmanian ferry sailed **straight** out through the heads and met rough seas in Bass **Strait**.

suede, swayed

The **suede** boots were so beautiful that Puss-in-Boots danced around and **swayed** with delight.

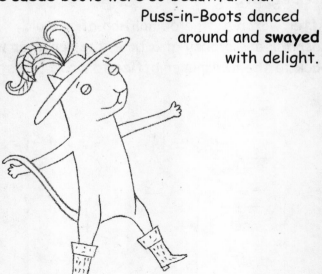

suite, sweet

When Mrs Rabbit moved the lounge **suite** to vacuum, she found a sticky **sweet** stuck to the carpet.

sundae, Sunday

Every **Sunday** after church the family would go to the café and have an ice-cream **sundae** as a treat.

Tt

tacks, tax

The Man in the Moon was shocked when a huge **tax** bill was pinned to his front door with **tacks**.

tail, tale

There's an old **tale** that if you pull the **tail** off a lizard it grows another — or maybe it's true.

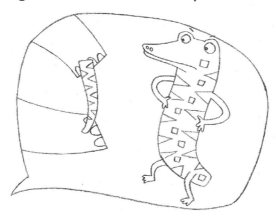

taught, taut, torte

With the microphone cord pulled **taut** to reach the cooking bench, Jiminy **taught** the audience how to make a chocolate **torte**.

te, tea, tee

Thumbelina drank herbal **tea** out of the top of
a golf **tee** and then practised her scales,
singing doh-ray-me-fah-soh-lah-**te**-doh.

doh-ray-me-fah-soh-lah-te-doh

team, teem

Heavy rain began to **teem** down
just as the football **team**
ran onto the oval.

teas, tease, tees

To **tease** the guests at the Queen of Hearts'
party, the Mad Hatter kept
hitting golf **tees** into
their **teas**.

their, there, they're

They're sure to find the way **there** using
their GPS.

threw, through

Because he was jealous, Aladdin's servant **threw** the amazing lamp **through** the open window.

throne, thrown

The King was sitting on his **throne** when a roll of toilet paper was **thrown** over the top of the door.

thyme, time

During an ad break, the famous TV chef had **time** to pick a handful of **thyme** from his herb garden.

tide, tied

Before the **tide** came in, Peter Pan rescued Tiger Lily who was **tied** to the pier.

tire, tyre

The support crew began to **tire** as they changed the racing car's **tyre** for the tenth time that day.

to, too, two

Those **two** are already champion pool swimmers and now they're off **to** the beach, hoping they'll win a triathlon **too**.

toad, towed

Out on the river the silly old **toad** lost his oars and had to be **towed** back to shore.

toe, tow

When he got a puncture, Ben tied a rope to his **toe** and started to **tow** his bike along behind him.

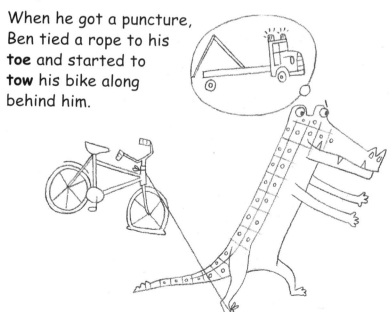

told, tolled

It was so late when the court jester had **told** his final tale for the night that the palace bells **tolled** midnight.

tracked, tract

By following the footprints on the **tract** of sand, the scouts **tracked** down the lost marathon runner.

troop, troupe

The dance **troupe** performed at the memorial service to honour the **troop** of soldiers who had died in the war.

Vv

vain, vane, vein

Showing off on the weather **vane**, the **vain** rooster crowed so loudly that he burst a **vein** in his throat.

verses, versus

Little Miss Muffet **versus** Little Jack Horner was the highlight of the poetry competition, with Jack winning because he recited the most **verses**.

vial, vile

It was the best show-and-tell ever because Pinocchio brought a **vial** full of **vile** gases that smelt like rotten eggs.

Ww

wade, weighed

Angus had to **wade** around in the dam until he was **weighed** down by enough yabbies to feed everyone for dinner.

wail, whale

When the Big Green **Whale** turned pink, he began to **wail**, fearing that he would never, ever be green again.

waist, waste

Old King Cole looked at his oversized **waist** and, realising he had no time to **waste**, started a diet immediately.

wait, weight

The crowd had to **wait** until the racing steward checked the winner's **weight** on the scales.

war, wore

Because he didn't want to fight in the **war**, the soldier **wore** a ballerina's tutu, hoping he'd be sent home.

ware, wear, we're, where

We're all going to **wear** our old fairy wings to the costume **ware**house, **where** we'll each buy a sparkling new pair.

warn, worn

The umpire had to **warn** the spin bowler that his fancy shoes must not be **worn** on the cricket pitch.

wax, whacks

The maid **whacks** the
rug as hard
as she can, but
is unable to get the
candle **wax** off it.

way, weigh, whey

The best **way** to eat curds and **whey** is to
weigh ten grams of it and then add twice as
much honey.

we, wee, whee

Wee Willie Winkie was so small that when he did a **wee** in the street and yelled '**Whee, whee, whee!**', **we** had to laugh.

weak, week

The Big Green Whale was so **weak** after he turned pink that he spent a **week** in bed until he was green again.

weal, we'll, wheel

We'll have to be very careful next time because the spinning **wheel** has left a nasty **weal** on your arm.

weather, wether, whether

When the **weather** turned nasty, Little Bo Peep wasn't sure **whether** to search for her lost **wether** or look after the rest of her flock.

weave, we've

Once **we've** spun the Golden Fleece, Jason can **weave** it into a coat for the dragon.

we'd, weed, weed

We'd been told that if we **weed** on the orange tree it would flourish, but all that flourished was one **weed**.

which, witch

In the ugliest-**witch** competition it was difficult to tell **which witch** was **which**.

whine, wine

Everyone heard the Wicked Witch **whine** when her special brew didn't win the gold medal at the **wine** show.

whirled, world

Erin **whirled** around the ice rink, dreaming of being **world** champion.

whirred, word

The robot's brain **whirred** for several minutes until it found the right **word** to greet the visitors from outer space.

who's, whose

Who's going to care **whose** porridge this is?
thought Goldilocks as she helped herself.

wood, would

Next time Miss Hood went to collect **wood**
for the fire, she **would** not wear her red
woollen coat.

Yy

yoke, yolk

When the ox broke free of the **yoke**, the cart stopped so suddenly that the dinosaur egg broke open, spilling its precious **yolk**.

yore, your, you're

You're sure to win the
fancy-dress prize with
your caveman costume
from days of **yore**.

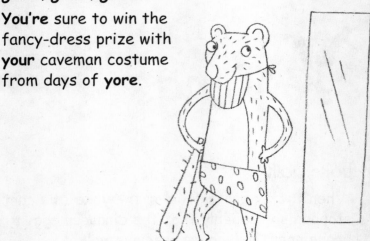

you'll, Yule

'I hope **you'll** all have a really cool **Yule**!' said
the Big Green Whale as he decorated his
Christmas tree.

homophone meanings

Notes:

One word may have several meanings. In this book you will find the meaning that relates to the way a word is used in its sentence.

The following groups of homophones are listed alphabetically according to the spelling of their first word.

The words within each group are then arranged alphabetically.

Abbreviations

adj.	adjective
adv.	adverb
conj.	conjunction
interj.	interjection
n.	noun
prep.	preposition
pron.	pronoun
v.	verb

Aa

ad *n.* abbreviation of "advertisement": a notice about things for sale
  add *v.* to put two or more things together

addition *n.* an extra inclusion
  edition *n.* copies of a newspaper (or book) printed at the same time

affect *v.* to influence
  effect *n.* a result

aisle *n.* a space for walking between rows of seats (or shelves)
  I'll contraction of "I will"
  isle *n.* a small island: a piece of land surrounded by water

allowed *v.* past participle of the verb "to allow": permit
  aloud *adv.* so it can be heard

altar *n.* a raised table for worship
  alter *v.* to change

ate *v.* past tense of the verb "to eat": consume by mouth
  eight *n.* the number after seven and before nine

awe *n.* fearful respect
  oar *n.* a long-handled pole with a flat end used to row a boat
  or *conj.* a word that connects alternative ideas
  ore *n.* minerals from the earth

aye *adv.* "yes" in sailor language
  eye *n.* the organ of sight
  I *pron.* first person singular; oneself

Bb

bail *n.* money to guarantee accused will return to court for trial
  bale *n.* a compact bundle tied with wire

bald *adj.* hairless
  bawled *v.* past tense of verb "to bawl": cry loudly

ball *n.* a spherical object used in sport
  bawl *v.* to cry loudly

band *n.* a flat strip of material for binding
  band *n.* a group of people or musicians
  banned *v.* past participle of verb "to ban": not allow

bare *adj.* without a covering
  bear *n.* a large hairy mammal with a short tail
  bear *v.* to tolerate

base *n.* the bottom of something
  bass *adj.* pitched low

be *v.* to exist
  bee *n.* a stinging insect

beach *n.* the sand next to the sea
  beech *n.* a deciduous Northern Hemisphere tree

bean *n.* a legume (vegetable)
  been *v.* past participle of the verb "to be": exist

beat *v.* to stir vigorously
  beet *n.* a dark red root used as a vegetable

berry *n.* a small stoneless fruit
  bury *v.* to put into the ground

berth *n.* a place where boats are moored
  birth *n.* the act of being born

bight *n.* an inward curve in the coastline
  bite *n.* a cut made with teeth
  byte *n.* a unit of information in computer language

billed *v.* past participle of the verb "to bill": charge for
build *v.* to make or construct

blew *v.* past tense of the verb "to blow": puff out air
blue *adj.* a primary colour, like the sky

boar *n.* a wild pig
bore *v.* to drill holes
bore *n.* a person who is dull

board *n.* a flat piece of wood or similar material
bored *adj.* tired because of a dull situation

boarder *n.* someone who pays for hospitality
border *n.* the line separating one country from another

bold *adj.* fearless
bowled *v.* past tense of the verb "to bowl": roll along the ground

bolder *adj.* braver
boulder *n.* a large rock

bough *n.* a branch of a tree
bow *n.* the act of bending over from the waist to show appreciation

boy *n.* a young male person
buoy *n.* a fixed floating object used as a navigation mark or as a mooring

braid *n.* a strip of fabric used as trimming
brayed *v.* past tense of the verb "to bray": cry loudly like a donkey

brake *n.* a stopping pedal or handle
break *v.* to divide suddenly into bits

bread *n.* a loaf made of flour
bred *v.* past tense of the verb "to breed": produce offspring

brewed *v.* past tense of the verb "to brew": make tea or coffee with boiling water
brood *n.* a group of siblings
brood *v.* to keep worrying about something

bridal *adj.* to do with a bride or a wedding
bridle *n.* the leather headgear used to control a horse

but *conj.* on the contrary
butt *v.* to push or hit someone (or something) with the head

buy *v.* to purchase
  by *prep.* indicates a means of doing something
  bye *n.* a sporting round with no opponent

Cc

calves *n.* plural of "calf": the back part of the lower leg
  calves *n.* plural of "calf": a cow or bull less than one year old
  carves *v.* present tense of the verb "to carve": slice cooked meat

caught *v.* past participle of the verb "to catch": grab or get
  court *n.* a level area for playing sport
  court *n.* a place where legal cases are heard

cause *n.* something that deserves people's support, such as a charity
  caws *n.* plural of "caw": the harsh cry of a crow

ceiling *n.* the overhead horizontal surface of a room
  sealing *v.* present participle of the verb "to seal": close up

cell *n.* a small room
  sell *v.* to give in exchange for money

cellar *n.* a room under a house
  seller *n.* a person who sells something

cent *n.* a unit of decimal money (one-hundredth of a dollar)
  scent *n.* a perfumed extract
  sent *v.* past tense of the verb "to send": cause to go away

cents *n.* plural of "cent": a coin
  scents *n.* plural of "scent": a smell

cereal *n.* processed grains to eat for breakfast
  serial *n.* a story in parts

cheap *adj.* not expensive
  cheep *n.* a bird noise, especially of chickens

chews *v.* present tense of the verb "to chew": grind with the teeth
  choose *v.* to select

Chile *n.* a South American country
  chilli *n.* a small, spicy, capsicum
  chilly *adj.* cold

choral *adj.* belonging to a choir
coral *n.* a substance formed from the skeletons of polyps in the ocean

chord *n.* three or more notes played together
cord *n.* a woven string
cored *v.* past tense of the verb "to core": remove the centre of something

chute *n.* a downward-sloping trough or tube
shoot *v.* to fire a missile

cite *v.* to quote
sight *n.* the ability to see, or something seen
site *n.* a location

Claus *n.* Santa
clause *n.* a section of a document
claws *n.* sharp, curved animal nails

coarse *adj.* rough
course *n.* a direction taken

colonel *n.* an army officer
kernel *n.* a seed or grain

complement *n.* something which completes something else
compliment *n.* an expression of praise

coo *n.* the soft sound made by pigeons
coup *n.* a sudden successful act

core *n.* the centre of something
corps *n.* a unit in the army

council *n.* an elected group that makes decisions
counsel *v.* to give advice

creak *v.* to make a squeaky noise
creek *n.* a small stream of water

crews *n.* plural of "crew": a group working together, especially on a ship or plane
cruise *n.* a journey on the ocean

cue *n.* a signal to do something
queue *n.* a line of people waiting

curb *v.* to pull back
kerb *n.* the edging between the footpath and the road

currant *n.* a small seedless raisin or grape
current *adj.* to do with the present time
current *n.* water moving in one direction

cymbal *n.* a brass plate used in a pair as a percussion instrument
symbol *n.* a representation of something

Dd

days *n.* plural of "day": a twenty-four-hour period
daze *n.* a stunned state of mind

dear *adj.* beloved; expensive
deer *n.* a hoofed mammal — the male has antlers

dew *n.* drops of moisture that condense from the air at night
due (to) *adj.* because of; owing or expected

died *v.* past tense of the verb "to die": pass away
dyed *v.* past participle of the verb "to dye": colour

discussed *v.* past participle of the verb "to discuss": talk about
disgust *n.* strong dislike

doe *n.* a female deer
doh *n.* the first and last note of the solfa musical scale
dough *n.* uncooked bread, cake or pastry

draft *n.* an early version of a written work
draught *n.* a gust of air

dual *adj.* having two parts
duel *n.* a contest between two people

Ee

earn *v.* to gain by working
urn *n.* a jar or container

ewe *n.* a female sheep
yew *n.* an evergreen European tree
you *pron.* second person singular and plural

ewes *n.* plural of "ewe": a female sheep
use *v.* to bring into action
yews *n.* plural of "yew": a European tree

Ff

faint *v.* to lose consciousness for a moment
feint *v.* to fake a move to confuse an opponent

fair *adj.* honest, within the rules; or of a light colour
fair *n.* a gathering where goods are bought and sold
fare *n.* a payment for transport

farther *adv.* at a greater distance
  father *n.* a male parent

fate *n.* destiny
  fête *n.* a fundraising fair

faux *adj.* not real
  foe *n.* an enemy

faze *v.* to upset
  phase *n.* a stage of development

feat *n.* an accomplishment
  feet *n.* plural of "foot": the part of the leg below the ankle, on which one stands

few *adj.* not many
  phew *interj.* an exclamation of discomfort

find *v.* to locate
  fined *v.* past participle of the verb "to fine": made to pay for a mistake

fir *n.* an evergreen tree with needle-like leaves
  fur *n.* fine, soft, animal hair

flair *n.* a talent for something
  flare *n.* a device to give a strong light, used as a distress signal

flaw *n.* a fault
  floor *n.* the underfoot horizontal surface of a room

flea *n.* a small insect that sucks blood
  flee *v.* to leave in a hurry

flecks *n.* plural of "fleck": a tiny fragment
  flex *v.* to bend or stretch

flew *v.* past tense of the verb "to fly": move through the air on wings
  flu *n.* abbreviation of "influenza": an infectious viral disease
  flue *n.* a chimney pipe

flour *n.* grain which has been ground into powder
  flower *n.* the decorative bloom on a plant

for *prep.* used to indicate purpose
  fore *n.* the front
  four *adj.* the number between three and five

fort *n.* abbreviation of "fortress": a building strengthened for defence
  fought *v.* past tense of the verb "to fight": struggle or contest

forth *adv.* forward in time or place
fourth *adj.* placed between third and fifth

foul *adj.* offensive
fowl *n.* a domestic hen

frees *v.* present tense of the verb "to free": let out
freeze *v.* to change into ice, become solid
frieze *n.* a decorative strip on a wall

Gg

gait *n.* any way of stepping along
gate *n.* a door in a fence

genes *n.* plural of "gene": the hereditary unit in a chromosome responsible for personal characteristics
jeans *n.* denim pants

gilt *adj.* gold-plated
guilt *n.* the feeling of being responsible for a mishap

gnaw *v.* to keep on chewing something
nor *conj.* used as a second negative, meaning "and not"

grade *n.* a group at the same level, such as a school class
greyed *v.* past tense of the verb "to grey": lose colour and fade to white

grate *v.* to shred
great *adj.* very good

graze *v.* to wander around eating grass
greys *n.* plural of "grey": a shade between black and white

grease *n.* an oily substance
Greece *n.* a country on the Mediterranean Sea

grill *v.* to cook one side at a time
grille *n.* a metal grating

groan *v.* to make a sound of discontent or pain
grown *v.* past participle of the verb "to grow": become larger

groin *n.* the place where the thigh joins the body
groyne *n.* a breakwater made from rocks

guessed *v.* past participle of the verb "to guess": form an opinion without facts
guest *n.* a visitor

gym *n.* an exercise room
  Jim *n.* abbreviation of the name "James"

Hh

hail *n.* frozen drops of rain
  hale *adj.* strong and healthy

hair *n.* growth of threads on skin
  hare *n.* an animal like a large rabbit

hall *n.* a corridor; a large room that holds lots of people
  haul *v.* to pull or drag along

hangar *n.* a building where planes are kept
  hanger *n.* a device on which to hang clothes

hay *n.* cut grass used as feed for animals
  hey *interj.* a greeting

heal *v.* to get well
  heel *v.* to walk next to one's heel, the back part of the foot
  he'll contraction of "he will"

hear *v.* to learn by listening — with the ear!
  here *adv.* in this place

heard *v.* past tense of the verb "to hear": learn by listening
  herd *n.* a group of animals

hi *interj.* a greeting
  high *adv.* far above the ground

higher *adv.* further up
  hire *v.* to pay to borrow something

him *pron.* the form of "he" that follows a verb or preposition
  hymn *n.* a song of praise

hoard *n.* a carefully saved store of something
  horde *n.* a crowd

hoarse *adj.* with a rough or failing voice
  horse *n.* a four-legged, solid-hoofed mammal

hoes *n.* plural of "hoe": a tool for scraping up weeds
  hose *n.* a tube to convey water

hold *v.* to keep
  holed *v.* past tense of verb "to hole": put a hole in something

hole *n.* a gap or opening in something
  whole *adj.* all of something

holey *adj.* with holes in it
holy *adj.* of religious importance
wholly *adv.* completely

hour *n.* sixty minutes
our *possessive adj.* belonging to us

humerus *n.* an arm bone
humorous *adj.* funny

Ii

idle *adj.* not busy, doing no work
idol *n.* a person who is adored

in *prep.* indicating time, place or situation
inn *n.* a small hotel

it's contraction of "it is"
its *possessive adj.* belonging to something

Jj

jam *n.* a spread made from fruit
jamb *n.* the upright side of a door frame

Kk

key *n.* an instrument for opening locks
quay *n.* a wharf or mooring place for ships

knead *v.* to work dough with the hands
need *v.* to require because it's important

knew *v.* past tense of the verb "to know": learn and remember
new *adj.* never used, recently made

knight *n.* a medieval nobleman, entitled to be called "Sir"
night *n.* the time after sunset and before sunrise

knit *v.* to make a garment by looping yarn together, especially wool
nit *n.* a tiny insect that lives in the hair of people and animals

knot *n.* a knob where cords or threads are tied
not *adv.* a word to express denial

know *v.* to learn and remember
no *adj.* not any

knows *v.* present tense of the verb "to know": learn and remember
noes *n.* plural of "no": a negative vote
nose *n.* the organ used to smell and breathe

Ll

lacks *v.* present tense of the verb "to lack": be without
lax *adj.* not strict enough

law *n.* a country's system of rules
lore *n.* traditional beliefs passed on by word of mouth

lays *v.* present tense of the verb "to lay": put something down
laze *v.* to be idle, not work
leis *n.* plural of lei: a floral necklace

lead *n.* a metal
led *v.* past tense of the verb "to lead": guide by going first

leak *v.* to lose liquid
leek *n.* a long vegetable, a bit like an onion

leant *v.* past tense of the verb "to lean": rest against
lent *v.* past participle of the verb "to lend": give on loan
Lent *n.* the forty days of fasting leading up to Easter

leased *v.* past tense of the verb "to lease": rent out for money
least *n.* the smallest amount

lessen *v.* to reduce
lesson *n.* a unit of teaching

liar *n.* someone who tells untruths
lyre *n.* a stringed instrument from Ancient Greece

licence *n.* a permit document
license *v.* to give permission to do something

lightening *v.* present participle of the verb "to lighten": make less heavy
lightning *n.* a flash of light in the sky during a thunderstorm

loan *n.* the act of borrowing something
lone *adj.* on one's own

loch *n.* a lake
lock *v.* to fasten, usually with a key

Mm

made *v.* past tense of the verb "to make": create; cause to be
maid *n.* old-fashioned word for a girl or a female servant

mail *n.* letters and parcels delivered to addresses
male *adj.* masculine in gender

main *adj.* the most important
mane *n.* the long hair on the necks of animals, especially horses

maize *n.* a grain crop
maze *n.* a confusing network of paths

manner *n.* the way something happens
manor *n.* a large estate

mare *n.* a female horse
mayor *n.* an elected leader of a city council

marshal *v.* to arrange in an orderly fashion
martial *adj.* warlike

meet *v.* to come face-to-face with someone
meat *n.* the flesh of an animal eaten as food

medal *n.* a small metal disc given as an award
meddle *v.* to interfere

meter *n.* an instrument to measure something
metre *n.* the base decimal unit of length measurement

might *v.* part of the auxiliary verb "may", used to express a possibility
mite *n.* a small creature or person

mind *v.* to feel troubled
mined *v.* past tense of the verb "to mine": dig for minerals

miner *n.* a person who works in a mine
minor *adj.* not important, small
mynah *n.* an Asian bird that mimics other birds

missed *v.* past tense of the verb "to miss": feel regret at someone's absence
mist *n.* a light fog

moan *n.* a long, low sound of pain
mown *v.* past participle of the verb "to mow": cut (grass or crops) with a machine

mode *n.* a method
mowed *v.* past tense of the verb "to mow": cut (grass or crops) with a machine

moor *n.* a wild area of land
more *adj.* additional

morning *n.* the time between sunrise and noon
mourning *n.* the expression of sorrow when remembering the dead

muscle *n.* the tissue in bodies that contracts to produce movement
mussel *n.* an aquatic bivalve mollusc, some of which are edible

mustard *n.* a spicy yellow sauce
mustered *v.* past tense of the verb "to muster": gather together

Nn

naval *adj.* to do with the Navy
navel *n.* the belly button

none *pron.* not any
nun *n.* a woman belonging to a religious order

Oo

ode *n.* a poem of praise
owed *v.* past tense of the verb "to owe": have a duty to do or give something

officers *n.* plural of "officer": a person of rank and authority
offices *n.* plural of "office": a room for professional work

oh *interj.* an exclamation expressing emotion, especially surprise
owe *v.* to have a duty to do or give something

one the lowest number; a single unit
won *v.* past tense of the verb "to win": be victorious

Pp

paced *v.* past tense of the verb "to pace": walk with steady steps
paste *n.* a thick glue

packed *v.* past tense of the verb "to pack": put in a container
pact *n.* an agreement

pail *n.* an old-fashioned word for a bucket
pale *adj.* light in colour

pain *n.* a distressing feeling somewhere in the body
pane *n.* a sheet of glass in a window or door

pair *n.* two of something
pare *v.* to trim by cutting off the outer layer
pear *n.* a fruit with a rounded base, thinner towards the stem

passed *v.* past tense of the verb "to pass": go by
past *n.* the time before now

pause *v.* to stop temporarily
paws *n.* plural of "paw": an animal's foot

paw *n.* an animal's foot
poor *adj.* having little money or goods
pore *n.* a tiny opening in the surface of the skin
pour *v.* to flow strongly

pea *n.* a green vegetable having seeds in a pod
pee *v.* colloquial: to urinate

peace *n.* freedom from strife or war
piece *n.* a section of something

peak *n.* the highest point
peek *n.* a quick look
pique *v.* to cause resentment

peal *n.* a prolonged sound
peel *n.* the skin of a fruit

pearl *n.* a gem formed in an oyster shell
purl *adj.* describing a stitch used in knitting

pedal *v.* to move by pushing down on the foot controls (pedals) of a bicycle
peddle *v.* to sell

peer *v.* to look hard in an attempt to see something
pier *n.* a wharf

plain *adj.* not fancy
plane *n.* abbreviation of the word "aeroplane"

pleas *n.* plural of "plea": a cry for help
please *v.* to make happy

pole *n.* a tall, thin, rounded post
poll *n.* a vote to test opinion

practice *n.* repeated effort to improve a skill
practise *v.* to work at something repeatedly so as to improve

praise *v.* to express approval
prays *v.* present tense of the verb "to pray": ask God for something

pray *v.* to ask God for something
prey *n.* animals and birds that are hunted as food

principal *n.* the head of a school
principle *n.* a basic rule or policy

profit *n.* a financial gain
prophet *n.* a person regarded as an inspired teacher sent by God

Rr

racket *n.* a loud noise
racquet *n.* a long-handled bat with strings for hitting a ball

rain *n.* water that falls from the sky
reign *n.* the period of a sovereign's rule
rein *n.* a long strip of leather on a bridle, used to control a horse

raise *v.* to move upwards
rays *n.* plural of "ray": a beam of light
raze *v.* to tear down completely

rapped *v.* past tense of the verb "to rap": knock sharply
rapt *adj.* full of delight
wrapped *v.* past tense of the verb "to wrap": enclose with a covering

raw *adj.* not cooked
roar *n.* a loud, prolonged sound

read *v.* past tense of the verb "to read": understand the written word
red *adj.* a primary colour, like fresh blood

read *v.* to understand the written word
reed *n.* the stalk of a tall grass

real *adj.* true, not false or imaginary
reel *n.* a cylinder on which to wind fishing line

reek *v.* to smell bad
wreak *v.* to inflict something unpleasant

right *adj.* correct
rite *n.* a ritual or solemn ceremony
write *v.* to form words or symbols on a page

ring *n.* a circular band worn on a finger
wring *v.* to twist and squeeze

road *n.* a surface made for vehicles
rode *v.* past tense of the verb "to ride": be carried on a conveyance
rowed *v.* past tense of the verb "to row": propel a boat by oars

roam *v.* to wander about
Rome *n.* the capital city of Italy

role *n.* a part to play
roll *v.* to move by turning over and over

root *n.* the part of a plant that's usually underground
route *n.* the way planned for travel

rose *n.* a garden shrub with thorns and fragrant flowers
rows *n.* plural of "row": a number of things or people arranged in a line

rote *n.* memorisation by repetition
wrote *v.* past tense of the verb "to write": form words on a page

rough *adj.* having an uneven or coarse surface
ruff *n.* a pleated collar

rung *n.* a step on a ladder
wrung *v.* past tense of the verb "to wring": twist and squeeze

Ss

sacks *n.* plural of "sack": a large, strong bag
sax *n.* abbreviation of "saxophone": a wind instrument

sail *v.* to travel in a wind-powered boat
sale *n.* the selling of goods at a reduced price

sauce *n.* a thickened liquid served with food
source *n.* where something comes from

saw *v.* past tense of the verb "to see": look with your eyes
soar *v.* to fly upwards or glide in the air
sore *adj.* physically painful

scene *n.* the place where something happens
seen *v.* past participle of the verb "to see": look with your eyes

sea *n.* the salt water that covers much of the earth
see *v.* to look with your eyes

seam *n.* a row of stitches that joins two pieces of fabric
seem *v.* to appear to be

seas *n.* plural of "sea": the salt water that covers much of the earth
sees *v.* present tense of the verb "to see": look with your eyes
seize *v.* to grab by force

sew *v.* to use needle and thread to join fabric
so *conj.* in order that
soh *n.* the fifth note of the solfa scale
sow *v.* to plant seeds

shear *v.* to clip wool off an animal
sheer *adj.* steep

shoe *n.* footwear
shoo *interj.* an exclamation used to make someone or something go away

shore *n.* the land along the edge of a sea or lake
sure *adj.* certain

side *n.* one of the surfaces bounding something
sighed *v.* past tense of the verb "to sigh": let out an audible breath

sighs *n.* plural of "sigh": an audible outward breath, often expressing a feeling
size *n.* how big something is

slay *v.* to kill
sleigh *n.* a carriage pulled by animals over snow

soared *v.* past tense of the verb "to soar": fly upwards or glide in the air
sword *n.* a long-bladed weapon

sold *v.* past tense of the verb "to sell": exchange for money
soled *v.* past tense of the verb "to sole": fit the bottom (sole) onto a shoe

sole *adj.* only
soul *n.* the spiritual part of a person; also an affectionate word for a person

some *adj.* describing something or someone unknown
sum *n.* a mathematical problem

son *n.* a male child
sun *n.* the star around which the earth revolves

sort *n.* a particular type
sought *v.* past tense of the verb "to seek": look for

spade *n.* a long-handled digging tool
spayed *v.* past participle of the verb "to spay": de-sex a female animal

stair *n.* a step
stare *v.* to look steadily at something

stake *n.* a pointed stick driven into the ground
steak *n.* a thick slice of meat

stationary *adj.* not moving
stationery *n.* office and school supplies, such as paper and pens

steal *v.* to take what's not yours
steel *n.* a tough form of iron

storey *n.* any of the levels of a building above the ground
story *n.* a narrative

straight *adv.* in one direction, without swerving
strait *n.* a narrow strip of water

suede *n.* a soft leather with a downy surface
swayed *v.* past tense of the verb "to sway": swing from side to side

suite *n.* a set of things
sweet *n.* a lolly

sundae *n.* a serve of ice-cream with sauce, nuts and cream
Sunday *n.* the first day of the week

Tt

tacks *n.* plural of "tack": a short nail with a large flat head
tax *n.* money paid to the government by citizens who earn an income

tail *n.* a flexible extension from an animal's back
tale *n.* a story

taught *v.* past tense of the verb "to teach": instruct
taut *adj.* pulled tight
torte *n.* a cake or tart

te *n.* the seventh note of the solfa scale
tea *n.* a drink made from dried leaves
tee *n.* a peg off which a golf ball is hit

team *n.* a group of people doing something together
teem *v.* to rain heavily

teas *n.* plural of "tea": a drink made from dried leaves
tease *v.* to annoy
tees *n.* plural of "tee": a peg off which a golf ball is hit

their *possessive adj.* belonging to them
there *adv.* in, at or to a particular place away from here
they're contraction of "they are"

threw *v.* past tense of the verb "to throw": send through the air by force
through *prep.* going in one side and out the other

throne *n.* a raised chair for an important person; slang name for a toilet
thrown *v.* past participle of the verb "to throw": send through the air by force

thyme *n.* a fragrant herb whose leaves are used in cooking
time *n.* the system for expressing when events happen and how long they last

tide *n.* the rise and fall of the surface of the sea
tied *v.* past tense of the verb "to tie": fasten with rope or something similar

tire *v.* to run out of energy or patience
tyre *n.* the rubber rim around a wheel

to *prep.* in the direction of
too *adv.* as well, also
two the second number; one plus one

toad *n.* an amphibian animal similar to a frog
towed *v.* past tense of the verb "to tow": pull along by a rope

toe *n.* a digit on a foot
tow *v.* to pull along by a rope

told *v.* past participle of the verb "to tell": give information
tolled *v.* past tense of the verb "to toll": sound (a bell) with slow regular strokes

tracked *v.* past tense of the verb "to track": follow and search
tract *n.* a large area of land

troop *n.* an assembled group, usually in the army
troupe *n.* a group of performers, usually a travelling one

Vv

vain *adj.* overly proud of one's looks or ability
vane *n.* a blade, fixed to a rotating axis, that moves in the wind
vein *n.* a tube that carries the body's blood back to the heart

verses *n.* plural of "verse": a section of a poem
versus *prep.* against

vial *n.* a small, rounded, glass container for holding liquid
vile *adj.* disgusting

Ww

wade *v.* to walk through water, with difficulty
weighed *v.* past participle of the verb "to weigh" (down): be heavy and cumbersome

wail *v.* to make a long, high-pitched sound to express emotion
whale *n.* a very large marine mammal

waist *n.* the part of the body between the ribs and the hips
waste *v.* to use carelessly

wait *v.* to stay without action until something happens
weight *n.* the heaviness of something

war *n.* armed conflict between nations
wore *v.* past tense of the verb "to wear": have on the body as clothing

ware *n.* a manufactured article offered for sale
wear *v.* to have on the body as clothing
we're contraction of "we are"
where *adv.* in or at which place

warn *v.* to tell someone in advance of a possible problem
worn *v.* past participle of the verb "to wear": have on the body as clothing

wax *n.* a solid form of certain oils
whacks *v.* present tense of verb "to whack": strike hard

way *n.* a method of doing something
  weigh *v.* to measure how heavy something is
  whey *n.* the watery part of milk that is left after the solid part (curd) is removed

we *pron.* first person plural; ourselves
  wee *adj.* Scottish word for tiny
  wee *n.* slang word for urination
  whee *interj.* an exclamation to express delight or movement

weak *adj.* not strong
  week *n.* a period of seven days

weal *n.* a raised mark on the skin
  we'll contraction of "we will"
  wheel *n.* a circular object that rotates on an axis

weather *n.* the climatic conditions
  wether *n.* a castrated male sheep
  whether *conj.* introduces a choice between alternatives

weave *v.* to make fabric by intertwining threads
  we've contraction of "we have"

we'd contraction of "we had"
  weed *n.* an unwanted plant
  weed *v.* past tense of the slang verb "to wee": urinate

which *adj.* what one (of things already mentioned)
  witch *n.* a woman who practises magic

whine *v.* to make a long, high-pitched sound of complaint
  wine *n.* an alcoholic drink made from grapes

whirled *v.* past tense of the verb "to whirl": spin rapidly
  world *n.* the earth and everything on it

whirred *v.* past tense of the verb "to whir": make a low, continuous spinning sound
  word *n.* the basic meaningful unit in speech or writing

who's contraction of "who is"
  whose *possessive adj.* belonging to whom

wood *n.* the trunks or branches of trees used as timber
would *v.* part of the auxiliary verb "will" used to express habit (in the past) or possibility (in the future)

Yy

yoke *n.* a crossbar with a looped end used to encircle the neck of a working animal
yolk *n.* the yellow centre of a bird's egg

yore *n.* long ago
your *possessive adj.* belonging to you
you're contraction of "you are"

you'll contraction of "you will"
Yule *n.* old-fashioned name for Christmas